DM-ID-2 Workbook

Rozemarijn Staal, Psy.D.

NADD An association for persons with developmental disabilities and mental health needs.

NATIONAL ASSOCIATION FOR THE DUALLY DIAGNOSED

132 Fair Street
Kingston, New York 12401

ISBN:978-1-57256-132-8
Printed in the United States of America

Acknowledgements

The idea to create a workbook that could accompany the then first edition of the *Diagnostic Manual-Intellectual Disability* came to me when I was trying to decide on a topic for my dissertation back in 2010, and completion of it wouldn't have been possible without Leon VandeCreek, Ph.D., ABPP who served as my Dissertation Chair, as well as Jeffery Allen, Ph.D., ABPP and Martin Moss, Ph.D. who served as Dissertation Committee Members. I also need to thank Roger Conn, Ph.D. who has played an integral role as mentor in my professional development as a graduate student and early career professional. Dr. Conn was kind enough to review the format and structure of the *DM-ID-2 Workbook* and to assist with a field trial of this tool. I would also like to thank Dr. Robert Fletcher as well as the members of the NADD Research Committee who took the time to review the *DM-ID-2 Workbook* and provide me with feedback prior to its publication.

Table of Contents

Purpose and Intended Use of the DM-ID-2 Workbook 1

Introduction 3

Overview of the DM-ID-2 Workbook 5

    Rationale for the Structure and Format 5

    DM-ID-2 Workbook Development Process 5

        Phase 1: Item Development 6

        Phase 2: Expert review of the DM-ID-2 Workbook 7

        Field Trial of the DM-ID-2 Workbook 7

        Expert Review by the NADD Research Committee 8

Administration 9

    Factors Clinicians Should Consider Prior to Starting the Evaluation 9

    Instructions for Using the DM-ID-2 Workbook 9

    The Structure and Organization of the DM-ID-2 Workbook 10

    Selection of Informants 10

    Ways in Which the Interview Questions Form Can Be Completed 11

    General Directions for Completing the Interview Questions Form 11

    The Significance of Looking at Both Baseline and Recent Behavior 12

    Completing the Scoring Sheet 12

    Using the Scoring Sheet and Decision Trees to Make a Diagnosis 12

    Abbreviated Instructions for Completing the Interview Questions Form 13

    Abbreviated Instructions for Completing the Scoring Sheet 14

    Abbreviated Instructions for Using the Scoring Sheet to Make a Diagnosis 14

DM-ID-2 Workbook Interview Questions 17

DM-ID-2 Workbook Scoring Sheets 31

DM-ID-2 Workbook Decision Trees 37

References 39

Purpose and Intended Use
of the DM-ID-2 Workbook

The *DM-ID-2 Workbook* was developed as an accompaniment to the *DM-ID-2* in order to provide clinicians such as physicians, psychologists, social workers, counselors, and therapists with a comprehensive method to use the adapted DSM-5 criteria found in the *DM-ID-2* to make an accurate diagnosis of mental illness in individuals who have an intellectual disability. The *DM-ID-2 Workbook* focuses on identifying observable signs of possible mental illness, particularly where symptom presentation and diagnostic criteria differ in individuals with ID. In doing so, this ensures that (a) all possible observable symptoms of psychopathology specific to individuals with ID that may have otherwise been misdiagnosed or overlooked are noted and incorporated into a diagnostic decision and (b) that all relevant diagnostic options are considered prior to making a diagnosis.

The *DM-ID-2 Workbook* was constructed as an informant-based, semi-structured interview so that the individual being assessed is not required to participate in the assessment procedure; instead, a respondent who is familiar with the individual's behavior can be asked to be an informant on the individual's behalf. However, the individual can serve as his or her own informant if collateral contacts are not available and in the evaluator's opinion the individual being assessed is a reliable informant. Potential informants include family members, staff members from the last or current placement, and mental health professionals such as a caseworker. The *DM-ID-2 Workbook* interview takes approximately 1 hour to complete with an informant. An additional 15 to 30 minutes is required to hand-score the workbook and complete the interpretive steps.

Introduction

Psychiatric disorders are common in individuals with intellectual disability (ID), but these disorders are often under or misdiagnosed (e.g. Gustafsson & Sonnander, 2004; Reiss, 1990). The diagnostic system that is currently used to diagnose mental illness in individuals with ID is the *Diagnostic and Statistical Manual of Mental Disorders - Fifth Edition* (DSM-5). This diagnostic system is designed for use with the general population (Poindexter, 1996) and is dependent upon an individual's ability to participate verbally during the evaluation process in order to diagnose psychopathology. Research has shown this becomes increasingly problematic as intellectual functioning level decreases (Rush & Frances, 2000). Individuals with ID can be nonverbal and therefore be unable to participate in the evaluation process through the self-report of symptoms. Research suggests that the symptoms of psychopathology may not be expressed in the same way in the ID population when compared to the general population due to lower intellectual functioning, learned behaviors, negative effects of institutionalization, or abnormal brain development (Moss et al., 1998), and that certain symptoms of psychopathology may not be expressed at all in individuals who are nonverbal (Moss, Emerson, Bouras & Holland, 1997). Further difficulty with using traditional diagnostic criteria lies in the fact that individuals with ID may lack insight into their own behavior and as a result are not always reliable self-reporters of the signs and symptoms that they are experiencing. For this reason, clinicians are often heavily dependent upon the caretaker's report of symptoms in order to make an accurate diagnosis, which may not be an unbiased account (Reiss, 1993). These factors have led clinicians to question the appropriateness and applicability of traditional diagnostic criteria, and the consensus is that the use of these traditional criteria becomes increasingly problematic the more severe the level of ID and the less the individual is able to participate in the diagnostic process. In short, research suggests that the existing diagnostic system is unable to diagnose psychopathology accurately in individuals with ID.

In order to facilitate a more accurate diagnosis of mental illness in individuals diagnosed with ID, NADD developed the *Diagnostic Manual - Intellectual Disability (DM-ID): A Textbook of Diagnosis of Mental Disorders in Persons with Intellectual Disability* (Fletcher, Loschen, Stavrakaki, & First, 2007) in association with the American Psychiatric Association (APA). Experts in the field adapted the diagnostic criteria of *DSM-IV-TR* utilizing an empirically based approach, which led to the development of a diagnostic system grounded in evidence-based methods, and supported by expert consensus, that reflects the current best clinical practice to diagnose psychiatric disabilities in persons with ID. A second edition to this manual has since been published by the NADD to reflect the changes made in the *DSM-5*. Like the first edition, the *DM-ID-2* provides clear examples of how symptom presentations can be interpreted and is designed with a developmental perspective in mind to help clinicians to recognize symptom profiles in adults with ID. Each diagnosis incorporates diagnostic considerations that highlight specific factors such as behavioral observations or environmental stressors that may need to be taken into consideration on a case-by-case basis prior to making a psychiatric diagnosis.

The *DM-ID-2 Workbook* was developed as an accompaniment to the *DM-ID-2* in order to assist clinicians to use the information provided in the *DM-ID-2* in a comprehensive way, as part of a comprehensive psychological evaluation, prior to making a diagnosis of mental illness in individuals with ID. The *DM-ID-2 Workbook* provides a structured interview format that focuses on observable behaviors where symptom presentation differs in individuals with ID. In doing so, this ensures that all possible observable symptoms of psychopathology specific to individuals with ID are noted and incorporated into a diagnostic decision. This is especially useful for clinicians who may not be very familiar with this population. Second, using this workbook ensures that all relevant diagnostic options are considered prior to making a diagnosis. In summary, the *DM-ID-2 Workbook* provides a comprehensive method to use the adapted *DSM-5* criteria found in the *DM-ID-2*, prior to making a diagnosis of mental illness in an individual with ID, increasing the likelihood that the most accurate and applicable diagnosis is made. An overview of the *DM-ID-2 Workbook* follows in the next chapter.

Overview of the
DM-ID-2 Workbook

Rationale for the Structure and Format

Expert consensus has found that a focus on behavioral observations rather than self-report of symptoms is a crucial part of making an accurate diagnosis in individuals who have an ID (Fletcher, Stravrakaki, Loschen & First, 2007). The use of a screening method that relies on behavioral observations eliminates the risk of denial or distortion from self-report of symptoms (Reis, 1993) and overcomes the difficulties that result from the limitations in the ability of individuals with ID to convey accurate information regarding symptoms either due to limited verbal ability or concrete cognitions (Einfield, 1992). Finally, the use of a tool that assists clinicians in making a reliable diagnosis will also eliminate the risk that data are based on acquiescence or the propensity to give socially acceptable answers, which individuals with ID often do (Einfield & Aman, 1995; Sovner & Pary, 1993). Research has shown that informant-based tools are more reliable than self-report tools with the ID population (Laman & Reis, 1987).

The *DM-ID-2 Workbook* was constructed as an informant-based, semi-structured interview so that the individual being assessed is not required to participate in the assessment procedure; instead, a respondent who is familiar with the individual's behavior can be asked to be an informant on the individual's behalf. However, the individual can serve as his or her own informant if collateral contacts are not available and, in the evaluator's opinion, the individual being assessed is a reliable informant. The *DM-ID-2 Workbook* provides a more complete picture of the individual's behavior prior to making a diagnosis, ensuring that no behavioral observations that are relevant to making a diagnosis are missed. A workbook that is specific to the *DM-ID-2* will assist the clinician in making a more accurate diagnosis of psychopathology in individuals with ID, thereby improving treatment of these individuals.

DM-ID-2 Workbook Development Process

The development of the *DM-ID-2 Workbook* began in 2010. The goal of creating this workbook was to aid clinicians in assessing the behavioral observations found specifically in individuals with ID, in order to help clinicians identify potential areas of diagnostic concern. The purpose of developing this workbook was to assist clinicians in gaining a complete picture of all relevant behaviors exhibited by the individual being assessed and to reduce the risk that key behavioral observations relevant to making an accurate diagnosis are missed. This workbook was designed to complement existing DSM diagnostic criteria. The *DM-ID* was selected as the source of information for the development of the items because it is designed specifically to diagnose psychopathology in individuals with ID, and it is the only diagnostic manual of its kind that is designed to be used with DSM criteria. In addition, the *DM-ID* is grounded in expert consensus and has clinical utility. Finally, literature postulates the importance of developing a tool that is informant-based rather than self-report based and that takes into consideration the observable behavioral symptoms indicative of psychopathology specific to this population.

The development of the workbook proceeded in three phases: the development of the items, a review of the workbook by experts, and the development of a user's manual. The two phases of instrument development and review are described in detail in the following sections. Once the *DM-ID-2* was published the workbook was updated to include the information provided in it.

Phase 1: Item Development

The first phase in the development of the *DM-ID-2 Workbook* involved the steps necessary for item preparation, which included both formulating and reviewing the items. The first step involved reviewing the *DM-ID* (Fletcher et al., 2007) in order to develop a comprehensive list of all behavioral observations, incorporating all the diagnostic categories described in the *DM-ID*. This list of behavioral observations was used to formulate the items. An effort was made to keep the wording of items closely tied to the *DM-ID* behavioral descriptors. These items were updated to include the changes made in the *DM-ID-2*.

The second step in the development of the items was to determine which diagnoses should, or should not, be incorporated in the workbook. The diagnostic categories selected were also updated as needed to include the changes made in the *DM-ID-2*. Several categories of disorders were omitted from this workbook because either no specific behavioral observations or very limited behavioral observations specific to individuals with ID were proposed by the *DM-ID-2*, making it unlikely that this diagnosis will be under or misdiagnosed in this population. The categories that were not incorporated for this reason include: (a) dissociative disorders, (b) somatic symptom and related disorders, (c) feeding and eating disorders, (d) elimination disorders, (e) sleep-wake disorders, (f) sexual dysfunctions, (g) gender dysphoria, (h) disruptive, impulse control, and conduct disorders, (i) substance-related and addictive disorders, (j) neurocognitive disorders, (k) personality disorders, and (l) paraphilic disorders. The elimination of these categories also ensured that the workbook remained user friendly in length. Attention deficit/hyperactivity disorder, reactive attachment disorder, and posttraumatic stress disorder domains were incorporated toward the end of the item development process in order to ensure differential diagnosis between these diagnoses and the diagnostic categories selected previously, due to the fact that symptom overlap was found between these diagnoses and the other diagnostic categories.

The third step in the development of the *DM-ID-2 Workbook* was to determine the structure of the domains and subdomains. Items were developed for the following diagnostic categories: (a) neurodevelopmental disorders, (b) schizophrenia and other psychotic disorders, (c) bipolar and related disorders, (d) depressive disorders, (e) anxiety disorders, (d) obsessive compulsive and related disorders, and (f) trauma and stressor-related disorders.

The fourth step in the item development process was to place the items into subdomains, until each subdomain was representative of a set of diagnostic criteria that corresponded to one or more disorders. To clarify, some subdomains or groups of items apply to more than one domain because of symptom overlap between diagnoses. For example, the subdomain or symptom of irritability can be found in the depressive disorders domain, anxiety disorders domain, and attention deficit and hyperactivity disorder/ post-traumatic stress disorder domain.

The scoring sheet illustrates how subdomains are grouped together to form domains (see page 31). The number of items developed for diagnostic categories ranged from 2 to 15 items per subdomain, dependent on the number of behavioral observations found in the *DM-ID-2*. Additional behavioral observations not mentioned in the *DM-ID-2* were not incorporated in order to ensure that the workbook focuses on observable behaviors where symptoms differ in individuals with ID (and may therefore be under or misdiagnosed). In addition, it is important that the tool is consistent with the current expert consensus in the field found in the *DM-ID-2* since this workbook is designed to be used as an accompaniment to the *DM-ID-2*.

Once the item list was created, the items were reviewed over the course of several months by the dissertation committee members and revised as needed until all items were clear and concise. The final version of the *DM-ID-2 Workbook* is composed of a total of 163 items and takes approximately one hour to complete (see page 17). Subdomains were grouped together until all the symptoms that make up the diagnoses applicable to that domain were incorporated (see page 31).

The final step in the development of the *DM-ID-2 Workbook* was to develop decision trees that incorporate all possible diagnostic options. These decision trees provide a list of possible diagnostic options. Each domain provides instructions on whether or not to turn to one or more decision trees, dependent upon the score obtained in each domain. If a set of symptoms could be representative of more than one diagnosis, this dilemma was resolved by incorporating another diagnosis on a particular decision tree, or pointing the clinician to more than one decision tree. The author chose a decision tree structure to ensure that clinicians were encouraged to consider all possible diagnostic options and make a differential diagnosis (see page 37).

Phase 2: Expert Review of the DM-ID-2 Workbook

According to the standards for educational and psychological testing, the test review process should involve a critique and use of the tool by an expert in the field who has the relevant qualifications and experience (American Educational Research Association, American Psychological Association, & National Council on Measurement in Education, 1999). The purpose of submitting this workbook to an expert was to get an opinion on the way it was designed in terms of length and structure and also to allow the opportunity to identify errors in the way that the questions in the workbook are posed, such as bias or convoluted wording of items. For this reason, the content validity was explored by submitting the *DM-ID-2 Workbook* to an expert in the field. The selection criteria for the expert in the field were that the person was a licensed clinical psychologist with at least ten years of experience assessing and diagnosing individuals with a dual diagnosis in clinical practice and that the person was not involved in the first phase of the tool development process.

The *DM-ID-2 Workbook* was submitted to Dr. Roger Conn, who is a licensed clinical psychologist with thirty-six years of experience working in the field of ID. This clinician did not find any inconsistencies with regard to the format and structure of the workbook and found that all items were worded clearly and concisely.

Field Trial of the DM-ID-2 Workbook.

According to the standards for educational and psychological testing, the items should be appropriate for the intended test takers (American Educational Research Association, American Psychological Association, & National Council on Measurement in Education, 1999). To ensure that wording was not too clinical or complicated, the same independent licensed clinical psychologist who reviewed the structure and format of the workbook, administered it with a direct care staff member at an Intermediate Care Facility for those with Intellectual Disabilities (ICF/ID). The clinician was asked to select a typical direct care staff member who had known the client for at least two weeks, and had time to answer all items in the workbook interview without distractions. Feedback from the expert was requested regarding the format and content of the items only, and no confidential client information was shared with the author of the workbook during this review process. The licensed clinical psychologist conducted the semi-structured interview with a direct care staff who spoke English as a second language, who had been employed at the ICF/ID facility for six years, and who worked closely with the client for one year. Only four items required further explanation during the administration procedure, namely items 103, 119, 128, and 153, because the informant did not understand some of the words used. The wording for these items was simplified in order to ensure that items could be easily understood by all intended informants.

In terms of selecting informants, it is recommended that administrators select informants who have some mental health training whenever possible. The field trial demonstrated that the items in this workbook can also be understood by informants who have received little or no mental health training such as family members and direct care staff, including those who do not speak English as a first language.

Expert Review by the NADD Research Committee

To explore content validity further, the next step in the workbook development process involved submitting the workbook to the Research Committee of the NADD. A total of nine experts reviewed the workbook, and feedback was provided. All the suggestions with regard to how the workbook could be improved were considered and evaluated in depth. There were no criticisms regarding the way items were phrased, nor were there any criticisms regarding the user manual of the *DM-D-2 Workbook*.

Administration

Factors Clinicians Should Consider Prior to Starting the Evaluation

Prior to beginning the evaluation, the clinician should insure that the examinee has had a complete medical evaluation within the last thirty days, and a dental exam, an eye exam, and a hearing exam within the last year whenever possible, to rule out any general medical conditions that may be affecting the examinee's observable behavior. If an organic brain injury is suspected, the individual's treating physician should be contacted to see if the examinee would benefit from a referral for a neurological evaluation. Obtaining an accurate and thorough developmental history can assist in identifying the presence of any general medical conditions.

Any unmet physical, occupational, or speech therapy needs should also be considered as possible causes of the examinee's observable behavior. For example, an inability to articulate in a way that caregivers understand can result in frustration or aggression on the part of the examinee. A speech device, speech therapy, or providing the examinee with the means to communicate via pictures could be possible solutions for those frustrations, and the behaviors should not be considered as evidence of a mental health disorder.

Clinicians should also consider whether behavior changes are the product of side effects of psychotropic medications, or whether these psychotropic medications are masking the presence of any observable behavioral symptoms that might be expected based on past diagnoses. In addition, clinicians should be willing to consider the possibility that prior diagnoses are medication-driven to control aggressive or non-compliant behavior. When there are questions with regard to the use of psychotropic medications, the treatment team should consult with the prescribing physician. It is often helpful for the treatment team to collaborate and clearly define the psychiatric symptoms that are the target of treatment with psychotropic medications and differentiate these from any target behaviors that are the focus of treatment with behavior supports. Any recent (and past history of) abuse, neglect, and/or trauma should also be considered when observing and evaluating the examinee's behavior. Examples of stressors include a move to a new placement, loss of independence, recent psychiatric hospitalization, and loss of a family member or friend, including death or loss of contact with loved ones. It is up to the clinician to determine whether any stressors are present that might account for the examinee's behavior.

Instructions for Using the DM-ID-2 Workbook

As mentioned previously, the *DM-ID-2 Workbook* was designed to help mental health professionals make a more accurate diagnosis of psychopathology in individuals with ID by reviewing all relevant observable behavioral symptoms. Items were developed utilizing behavioral symptoms indicative of psychopathology found in the *DM-ID-2*, and this workbook is designed to be used in conjunction with the adapted diagnostic criteria found in the *DM-ID-2*. Clinicians utilize the workbook by conducting a semi-structured interview with an informant who knows the examinee well. Obtaining the required information from the informant takes approximately one hour. An additional fifteen to thirty minutes is required to hand-score the tool and complete the interpretive steps. The workbook gathers information for both baseline and recent behavior. Baseline behavior is defined as behavior that has been consistent over six or more months. Recent behavior is defined as behavior that has changed or increased in intensity or frequency in the last two weeks.

The purpose of evaluating the individual's entire range of behavior is to ensure that behaviors relevant to specific diagnoses are not missed and that behavioral observations are not misinterpreted as psychopathology when a disorder is not present. It is important to note that this workbook only focuses on behavioral observations that research has shown to be different in persons with ID, in order to make this workbook as short and user friendly as possible. Several categories of disorders were omitted from this workbook because no specific behavioral observations, or very limited behavioral observations, specific to individuals with ID were proposed by the *DM-ID-2*, making it unlikely that this diagnosis would be under or misdiagnosed in this population. For this reason, this workbook focuses on a) neurodevelopmental disorders, (b) schizophrenia and other psychotic disorders, (c) bipolar and related disorders, (d) depressive disorders, (e) anxiety disorders, (d) obsessive compulsive and related disorders, and (f) trauma and stressor-related disorders. This means that clinicians should not ignore other symptoms indicative of psychopathology that are not highlighted in this workbook during the evaluation process.

The Structure and Organization of the DM-ID-2 Workbook

The *DM-ID-2 Workbook* includes 163 items. These items are grouped into 11 domains and 42 subdomains. The domains are: (a) depressive disorders, (b) mania or hypomania, (c) panic disorders, (d) anxiety disorders, (e) autism spectrum disorders, (f) stereotypic movement disorder, (g) tic disorders, (h) psychotic disorders, (i) attention deficit hyperactivity disorder, post-traumatic stress disorder, and acute stress disorder, (j) reactive attachment disorder, and (k) obsessive-compulsive disorder. Each domain is associated with one or more corresponding decision trees, which assist the clinician in making a differential diagnosis. There are a total of 11 decision trees. See figure 1 below for an overview of the structure of the *DM-ID-2 Workbook*. The scoring sheets provide an overview of the 11 domains and their corresponding subdomains (see page 31).

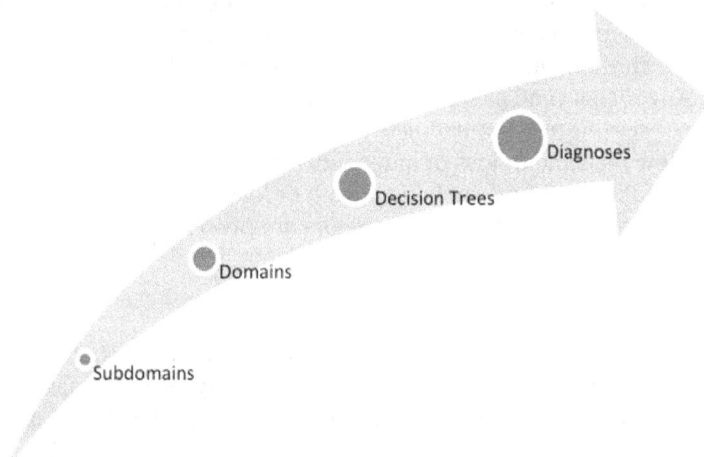

Figure 1. Structure of the *DM-ID-2 Workbook*.

The Selection of Informants

Ideally, an informant should have baseline and recent knowledge of the examinee's behavior and have had a relationship with the examinee for at least six months that has included spending a significant amount of time with the examinee. An informant who has had a relationship with the examinee for at least six months and remains actively involved with the examinee at the time of the evaluation should be able to answer questions regarding both baseline and recent behavior. Potential informants include family members, staff members from the last or current placement, and mental health professionals such as a caseworker. If one informant is not available to complete items regarding recent and baseline behavior, two separate informants can be used. Informants giving information about baseline behavior should have had a relationship with the examinee for at least six months. Informants giving information about recent behavior should have had an opportunity to familiarize themselves with the individual's behavior for at least two weeks.

Ways in Which the Interview Questions Form Can Be Completed

The *DM-ID-2* modified criteria rely heavily on observable behaviors of the individual rather than on examinee self-report. Consequently, clinicians will obtain the most accurate information about an examinee's behaviors from informants who have knowledge of the individual over at least a six-month period. Behaviors that may have begun recently for the individual during the past week or two, for example, may reflect temporary responses to unique stressors rather than the development of psychopathology. On the other hand, it is recognized that in some cases it may be impossible to find one good informant who has sufficient information about an individual's baseline (long standing) and recent behaviors. The clinician can use the workbook in one of three ways. (a) The clinician can gather information for both prior baseline and recent behavior items from one informant, if an informant is available who has knowledge of the examinee's recent and baseline behavior, and the informant has had a close relationship with the examinee for at least 6 months. (b) The clinician can complete the workbook survey in two interviews, if two separate informants are available that can give information regarding baseline and recent behaviors. (c) If no informants are available who can answer questions regarding baseline behavior, or there is insufficient time to perform two interviews due to system limitations, the clinician can complete the workbook interview with an informant who has knowledge of the examinee's recent behavior and has actively worked with this individual for at least two weeks and use that information to make a diagnosis. In addition, the clinician should investigate whether or not the observed behaviors are consistent across settings such as the home environment and sheltered employment, by observing the examinee's behavior in at least two settings or gathering information through clinical interviewing in at least two settings whenever possible.

It is recommended that the workbook results be reviewed within approximately six months to ensure that the diagnosis made is still accurate once the person has had a chance to adjust to whatever stressors might have been present if (a) the diagnosis was made solely on recent behavior and no informant was available who could provide information about baseline behavior, (b) the diagnosis was made based on gathering information through clinical interviewing at one setting, since ideally a diagnosis should be made by considering the client's behavior in more than one setting, and (c) if the examinee was influenced by current stressors when the initial evaluation was made, such as a move to a new placement within the last thirty days, loss of independence, or the death of a family member or friend, or the examinee had a change in contact with family or friends.

General Directions for Completing the Interview Questions Form

For your convenience, a printable or fillable PDF of the Interview Questions Form is available online at http://thenadd.org/dmid2wb.

For the purpose of completing the Interview Questions Form, a behavior is considered baseline (B) if the individual usually behaves in a certain way and this behavior has been consistent for at least six months. A behavior is considered recent (R) if it has changed in the last two weeks. Whenever possible, the clinician should score each item for both baseline and recent behavior.

If the examinee performs the behavior frequently, a score of "2" should be given. If the examinee performs the behavior sometimes, a score of "1" should be given, and if the examinee never performs the behavior, a score of "0" should be given, if the informant is unsure whether a particular behavior applies to the examinee, the clinician should circle the question mark "?" next to the scoring column and make a determination, if possible, based on observations or other sources, such as clinical records, to ensure that all items are addressed. Occasionally, information in the far right column entitled "notes" alerts the clinician to special considerations or instructions for scoring a particular subdomain or item.

The Significance of Looking at Both Baseline and Recent Behavior

By looking at both baseline and recent behavior, the clinician is able to gain a better understanding of how the examinee typically behaves and use the comparison between baseline and recent behavior to determine if there has been a change in this behavior. This allows the clinician to make a diagnosis based on a long-standing history of the examinee's behavior or to make a diagnosis based on a change in baseline behavior. Clear knowledge and understanding of baseline behavior has implications for understanding the effects of psychotropic medications, indicating whether a change in diagnosis is necessary, and/or helping the clinician determine if current treatment such as a behavior support plan, psychotherapy, or the use of psychotropic medication is having an effect on the examinee's observable behavior.

Completing the Scoring Sheet

For your convenience, a printable or fillable PDF of the Scoring Sheet is available online at http://thenadd.org/dmid2wb.

The first step in scoring involves adding up the 0-, 1-, and 2- point scores for each subdomain, and recording the total score at the end of each subdomain directly on the Interview Questions Form. In the second step, the total scores for each subdomain are transferred to the scoring sheet (see page 17). Some subdomains are listed on the scoring sheet under multiple domains. Clinicians should complete the entire scoring sheet until there are no blanks left. Score elevations are specific to each domain, and the scoring sheet indicates how many points are necessary in a given number of subdomains to be considered elevated. Each domain on the scoring sheet instructs the clinician when to turn to a decision tree based on the total score in a given number of subdomains.

Using the Scoring Sheet and Decision Trees to Make a Diagnosis

In order to assist clinicians in making a more accurate diagnosis in this population, the decision trees serve as a link between behavioral observations and likely psychiatric diagnoses based on observable behaviors specific to individuals with ID, (see page 37). As mentioned earlier, the behavioral observations covered in the *DM-ID-2 Workbook* only cover specific behavioral observations and possible psychiatric diagnoses that differ in individuals with ID compared to the general population and do not provide an all-inclusive list of all possible behavioral observations that are included in the *DM-ID-2*.

The decision trees are meant to serve as a guide for clinicians in order to ensure that behavioral observations that differ in this population are not overlooked or misinterpreted. The diagnoses obtained using the decision trees are not meant to be considered the only diagnostic options for the examinee, nor are they intended to be used without consulting the *DM-ID-2*. Clinicians must refer to the *DM-ID-2* diagnostic criteria to determine the best possible diagnosis for the examinee. Each decision tree has a list of diagnoses that may be relevant to the individual. Scores in subdomains can be used to make a differential diagnosis. The purpose of the decision trees is to highlight relevant clinical diagnoses and assist in making a differential diagnosis, but the task of making a specific diagnosis will be up to the discretion and clinical judgment of the clinician who can take into consideration the specific factors surrounding the examinee. If there is insufficient information to answer all the items utilizing informants, clinical records, or from observing behavior directly, caution should be exercised when making a diagnosis. It is recommended that the Interview Questions Form be completed again in six months' time to gather additional information.

The scoring sheet should be completed in its entirety prior to following the steps regarding decision trees, because there is overlap between certain subdomains and corresponding diagnoses. Once the scoring sheet has been completed, the clinician will be able to get an overview of elevations in the domains and determine which domains have the highest scores. The higher the score in a given domain, the more likely the corresponding decision tree(s) will list the most applicable diagnosis. Certain domains instruct the clinician to turn to more than one decision tree to ensure consideration of differential diagnoses. Subdomains and corresponding domains should be interpreted with caution if there are unanswered items. If an examinee's scores apply to multiple decision trees, this means that (a) more than one diagnosis is present or (b) the features of the given diagnoses overlap. In these instances, clinicians should use their own clinical judgment to determine which diagnosis best matches the observable behaviors of the examinee. In general, the higher an examinee scores in a given domain, the more likely it is that the most appropriate diagnosis is found in the corresponding decision tree(s). Clinicians should review each diagnosis indicated as a diagnostic option using the *DM-ID-2* and ensure that the diagnosis given meets diagnostic criteria prior to making a diagnosis. Clinicians should also pay particular attention to diagnoses that exclude one another, in order to ensure that the most accurate diagnosis is given and that the fewest possible number of diagnoses are given.

Abbreviated Instructions for Completing the Interview Questions Form

For your convenience, a printable or fillable PDF of the Interview Questions Form is available online at http://thenadd.org/dmid2wb.

Abbreviated instructions are provided here for ease of use. When completing the Interview Questions Form, note that a behavior is considered baseline (B) if the examinee usually behaves in a certain way and this behavior has been consistent for a significant length of time, preferably six months or more. A behavior is considered recent (R) if it has changed in the last two weeks.

When completing items, circle the option "2" if the examinee has performed or currently performs the behavior often, circle "1" when the examinee has performed or currently performs the behavior sometimes, and circle "0" if the examinee has never performed the behavior for baseline or current behavior according to the informant's knowledge. If the informant has no knowledge of the examinee's behavior, circle "DK" (don't know). If the informant is unable to respond to an item or the clinician is unsure whether the informant has an accurate understanding of an examinee's behavior, the clinician can circle the question mark '?' next to that item and make a determination on how to score that item based on clinical records, other informants, or clinical observation. Once the items have been scored, add up the 0s, 1s, and 2s for each subdomain to yield a total raw score for each subdomain.

Abbreviated Instructions for Completing the Scoring Sheet

For your convenience, a printable or fillable PDF of the Scoring Sheet is available online at http://thenadd.org/dmid2wb.

Transfer the total scores for each subdomain to the scoring sheets (see page 31). Some subdomains are listed on the scoring sheet under multiple domains. Clinicians should complete the entire scoring sheet until there are no blanks left. If there is insufficient information to complete the workbook in its entirety utilizing informants and clinical records, or from observing behaviors directly, caution should be exercised when making a diagnosis. It is recommended that the workbook procedure be completed again in less than one year to confirm the accuracy of the diagnosis or diagnoses made.

Abbreviated Instructions for Using the Scoring Sheet to Make a Diagnosis

Elevations are specific to each domain, and the scoring sheet indicates how many points are necessary in a given number of subdomains to be considered elevated. Scores in subdomains can be used to inform differential diagnosis. Each domain instructs the clinician whether to turn to a decision tree based on the total score in a given number of subdomains. Each decision tree has a list of diagnoses that may be relevant to the examinee (see page 37). The purpose of the decision trees is to highlight relevant clinical diagnoses and assist in making a differential diagnosis. Clinicians should note that the task of making a specific diagnosis will be up to their discretion and clinical judgment, taking into consideration the specific factors surrounding the examinee. Occasionally suggestions or diagnostic considerations will appear next to particular items in the adjacent column entitled 'notes' that the clinician should bear in mind while conducting the semi-structured interview or during the scoring process.

For your convenience,
printable and fillable PDFs of the
Interview Questions Form and the
Scoring Sheet are available online at
http://thenadd.org/dmid2wb

ROZEMARIJN STAAL, PSY.D.

DM-ID-2 Workbook
Interview Questions

Key to Response Options:

2 = Frequently, 1 = Sometimes, 0 = Never, DK = Don't Know,

B = Baseline Behavior that has been present or consistent for at least 6 months;

R = Behaviors that have been present in the last 2 weeks, or that are new or have changed in the last 2 weeks.

	Depression Subdomain			Notes: A high score in this category indicates a possible subtype of melancholic features.
1.	Looks or acts sad	(B) 2 1 0 DK; (R) 2 1 0 DK	?	
2.	Shows flat affect (little or no emotional expression)	(B) 2 1 0 DK; (R) 2 1 0 DK	?	
3.	Rarely smiles or laughs	(B) 2 1 0 DK; (R) 2 1 0 DK	?	
4.	Looks tearful or cries often	(B) 2 1 0 DK; (R) 2 1 0 DK	?	
				Total Score for Depression Subdomain (B) = ___ (R) = ___
	Irritability/Aggression Subdomain			Notes: DSM has included a new diagnosis, disruptive mood dysregulation disorder. Consider this diagnosis for children who have severe, non-episodic irritability that is developmentally inappropriate.
5.	Appears grouchy or has an angry facial expression	(B) 2 1 0 DK; (R) 1 2 0 DK	?	
6.	Engages in self-harming behavior (e.g., scratching or hitting self)	(B) 2 1 0 DK; (R) 2 1 0 DK	?	
7.	Engages in physical aggression towards others (e.g., hitting others, kicking others, or biting others)	(B) 2 1 0 DK; (R) 2 1 0 DK	?	
8.	Engages in disruptive behavior (e.g., oppositional or defiant)	(B) 2 1 0 DK; (R) 2 1 0 DK	?	
9.	Yells or swears at others	(B) 2 1 0 DK; (R) 2 1 0 DK	?	
10.	Engages in destructive behavior (e.g., damaging property)	(B) 2 1 0 DK; (R) 2 1 0 DK	?	
				Total for Irritability Subdomain (B) = ___ (R) = ___
	General Behavior Subdomain			Notes: None
11.	Refuses to participate in social, non-social, or preferred activities	(B) 2 1 0 DK; (R) 2 1 0 DK	?	
12.	Shows withdrawn behavior (e.g., spends a lot of time alone)	(B) 2 1 0 DK; (R) 2 1 0 DK	?	
13.	Responds with aggression to requests to participate in social activities	(B) 2 1 0 DK; (R) 2 1 0 DK	?	

14.	Exhibits anhedonia (does not appreciate things that most people find enjoyable such as favorite meals, objects, outings, or activities, or does not care about appearance)	(B) 2 1 0 DK; (R) 2 1 0 DK	?	
				Total for General Behavior Subdomain (B) = ___ (R) = ___
	Weight/Appetite Subdomain			Notes: None
15.	Eats to excess, or eats less than before	(B) 2 1 0 DK; (R) 2 1 0 DK	?	
16.	Obsesses over food or steals food	(B) 2 1 0 DK; (R) 2 1 0 DK	?	
17.	Refuses meals or tries to hide food	(B) 2 1 0 DK; (R) 2 1 0 DK	?	
18.	Shows clinically significant weight gain or loss	(B) 2 1 0 DK; (R) 2 1 0 DK	?	10% of body weight is clinically significant.
19.	Becomes agitated in relation to food or mealtimes (e.g., throws food on the floor)	(B) 2 1 0 DK; (R) 2 1 0 DK	?	
				Total for Weight/Appetite Subdomain (B) = ___ (R) = ___
	Insomnia/Hypersomnia Subdomain			Notes: None
20.	Has difficulty falling asleep, gets little sleep, or wakes up frequently during the night	(B) 2 1 0 DK; (R) 2 1 0 DK	?	
21.	Wakes up too early in the morning (without being woken up or using an alarm clock)	(B) 2 1 0 DK; (R) 2 1 0 DK	?	
22.	Takes frequent naps during the day or sleeps excessively	(B) 2 1 0 DK; (R) 2 1 0 DK	?	
23.	Shows problem behaviors late at night or early in the morning	(B) 2 1 0 DK; (R) 2 1 0 DK	?	
				Total for Insomnia/Hypersomnia Subdomain (B) = ___ (R) = ___
	Psychomotor Agitation Subdomain			Notes: None
24.	Rarely sits down, or gets up and sits down a lot	(B) 2 1 0 DK; (R) 2 1 0 DK	?	
25.	Paces or walks rapidly	(B) 2 1 0 DK; (R) 2 1 0 DK	?	
26.	Fidgets	(B) 2 1 0 DK; (R) 2 1 0 DK	?	
27.	Talks or makes noise excessively (e.g., inappropriate talk or talk that irritates others)	(B) 2 1 0 DK; (R) 2 1 0 DK	?	

			Total for Psychomotor Agitation Subdomain (B) = ___ (R) = ___	
	Psychomotor Retardation Subdomain		Notes: None	
28.	Moves slowly	(B) 2 1 0 DK; (R) 2 1 0 DK	?	
29.	Talks little, or speaks rarely	(B) 2 1 0 DK; (R) 2 1 0 DK	?	
30.	Engages in physical activity with reluctance	(B) 2 1 0 DK; (R) 2 1 0 DK	?	
			Total for Psychomotor Retardation Subdomain (B) = ___ (R) = ___	
	Fatigue/ Energy Loss Subdomain		Notes: None	
31.	Reports feeling tired or appears tired (e.g., yawning, dark circles under eyes)	(B) 2 1 0 DK; (R) 2 1 0 DK	?	
32.	Gets agitated or refuses when asked to participate in activities that require physical effort	(B) 2 1 0 DK; (R) 2 1 0 DK	?	
33.	Sits or lies down excessively	(B) 2 1 0 DK; (R) 2 1 0 DK	?	
			Total for Fatigue/Energy Loss Subdomain (B) = ___ (R) = ___	
	Feelings of Worthlessness/ Excessive or Inappropriate Guilt Subdomain		Notes: People with severe or profound ID may be unable to express feelings of guilt or worthlessness.	
34.	Has a negative attitude towards self (e.g., identifies self as a bad person or blames self inappropriately)	(B) 2 1 0 DK; (R) 2 1 0 DK	?	
35.	Expects to be punished when there is no history of being treated harshly	(B) 2 1 0 DK; (R) 2 1 0 DK	?	
36.	Has unrealistic fears of being rejected (fears that aren't real)	(B) 2 1 0 DK; (R) 2 1 0 DK	?	
37.	Needs excessive reassurance (excessive help to feel less afraid, upset, or doubtful)	(B) 2 1 0 DK; (R) 2 1 0 DK	?	
			Total for Worthlessness/Guilt Subdomain (B) = ___ (R) = ___	

Diminished Ability to Concentrate/ Distractibility Subdomain
Note: Score this category for either or both categories as applicable for examinee. Concentration is defined as the ability to give undivided attention. Distractibility is defined as being easily distracted by small and irrelevant stimuli.

Notes: When scoring this category determine if symptoms indicate difficulties with concentration or distractibility

		Concentration	Distractibility		
38.	Has difficulty performing up to ability at work or a day program	(B) 2 1 0 DK (R) 2 1 0 DK	(B) 2 1 0 DK (R) 2 1 0 DK	?	
39.	Has difficulty with or diminished self-care skills	(B) 2 1 0 DK (R) 2 1 0 DK	(B) 2 1 0 DK (R) 2 1 0 DK	?	
40.	Appears easily distracted	(B) 2 1 0 DK (R) 2 1 0 DK	(B) 2 1 0 DK (R) 2 1 0 DK	?	

41.	Has difficulty completing tasks that he or she is able to complete	(B) 2 1 0 DK (R) 2 1 0 DK	(B) 2 1 0 DK (R) 2 1 0 DK	?	
42.	Demonstrates agitated behavior when asked to do tasks that require concentration	(B) 2 1 0 DK (R) 2 1 0 DK	(B) 2 1 0 DK (R) 2 1 0 DK	?	
43.	Has memory problems that "come and go"	(B) 2 1 0 DK (R) 2 1 0 DK	(B) 2 1 0 DK (R) 2 1 0 DK	?	
44.	Shows an unexplained loss of skills or an uncharacteristic inability to learn new skills	(B) 2 1 0 DK (R) 2 1 0 DK	(B) 2 1 0 DK (R) 2 1 0 DK	?	
45.	Has difficulty with, or stopped attending, workshop programming or employment due to poor performance	(B) 2 1 0 DK (R) 2 1 0 DK	(B) 2 1 0 DK (R) 2 1 0 DK	?	
					Total for Concentration Subdomain (B) = ___ (R) = ___ Total for Distractibility Subdomain (B) = ___ (R) = ___
	Recurrent Thoughts of Death/Suicidal Ideation Subdomain				Notes:
46.	Talks about death, or people who have died, or has morbid preoccupations	(B) 2 1 0 DK; (R) 2 1 0 DK		?	
47.	Makes frequent unrealistic or unfounded physical complaints	(B) 2 1 0 DK; (R) 2 1 0 DK		?	
48.	Expresses fears of illness or death	(B) 2 1 0 DK; (R) 2 1 0 DK		?	
49.	Makes threats to kill or harm self or has attempted suicide	(B) 2 1 0 DK; (R) 2 1 0 DK		?	Suicidal attempts can involve unconventional and impulsive means (e.g. running in front of a car, jumping from a window).
					Suicidal Thoughts/Ideation Subdomain (B) = ___ (R) = ___
	Mania Subdomain				Notes: To give points, symptoms must last for at least one week, or any length of time if hospitalization was necessary.
50.	Laughs excessively loud, or sings during inappropriate times	(B) 2 1 0 DK; (R) 2 1 0 DK		?	
51.	Demonstrates excessive giddiness or silliness during inappropriate times	(B) 2 1 0 DK; (R) 2 1 0 DK		?	
52.	Demonstrates intrusiveness (e.g., getting into someone else's personal space)	(B) 2 1 0 DK; (R) 2 1 0 DK		?	
53.	Smiles excessively in ways not appropriate to social context	(B) 2 1 0 DK; (R) 2 1 0 DK		?	

54.	Demonstrates changeable mood that switches between excessive happiness and irritability	(B) 2 1 0 DK; (R) 2 1 0 DK	?	
				Total for Mania Subdomain (B) = ___ (R) = ___
	Inflated Self-Esteem/ Grandiosity Subdomain			Notes: Claims may represent wishes rather than mood congruent delusional beliefs.
55.	Exaggerates skills, stature, or accomplishments (e.g., makes claims that are not true)	(B) 2 1 0 DK; (R) 2 1 0 DK	?	
56.	Exaggerates social events (e.g., claims of an upcoming marriage when the person is not engaged)	(B) 2 1 0 DK; (R) 2 1 0 DK	?	
57.	Claims a relationship with a famous person or brief acquaintance	(B) 2 1 0 DK; (R) 2 1 0 DK	?	
58.	Believes that he or she is a super hero	(B) 2 1 0 DK; (R) 2 1 0 DK	?	Fantasy must not be consistent with examinee's mental age to score as 2 or 1.
				Total for Inflated Self Esteem/Grandiosity Subdomain (B) = ___ (R) = ___
	Decreased Need for Sleep Subdomain			Notes: Sleep problems should not be due to noise; person should not have a lifelong history of poor sleep; person should not be sleeping during the day. The sleep problem may resist treatment.
59.	Sleeps 0-3 hours at night (there may be minimal signs of fatigue)	(B) 2 1 0 DK; (R) 2 1 0 DK	?	
60.	Goes to sleep late or wakes early (may get ready for the day early)	(B) 2 1 0 DK; (R) 2 1 0 DK	?	
61.	Engages in behavioral problems or day time activities at night	(B) 2 1 0 DK; (R) 2 1 0 DK	?	
62.	Appears driven (a compulsive or urgent quality)	(B) 2 1 0 DK; (R) 2 1 0 DK	?	
				Total for Decreased Need for Sleep Subdomain (B) = ___ (R) = ___
	Talkativeness/Pressure to Talk Subdomain			Notes: Symptoms can be verbal or nonverbal.
63.	Vocalizes or talks often (e.g., screams, sings loudly, or makes verbal or non-verbal vocalizations)	(B) 2 1 0 DK; (R) 2 1 0 DK	?	
64.	Engages in nonstop or rapid vocalizations or monologues	(B) 2 1 0 DK; (R) 2 1 0 DK	?	
65.	Asks repeated questions without waiting for answers	(B) 2 1 0 DK; (R) 2 1 0 DK	?	
66.	Demonstrates a decreased ability to listen and/or interrupts frequently	(B) 2 1 0 DK; (R) 2 1 0 DK	?	
67.	Experiences, perseverations, flights of ideas, or says that thoughts are moving fast	(B) 2 1 0 DK; (R) 2 1 0 DK	?	
68.	Jumps from topic to topic	(B) 2 1 0 DK; (R) 2 1 0 DK	?	
				Total for Talkativeness Subdomain (B) = ___ (R) = ___

	Goal-Directed Activity Subdomain			Notes: None
69.	Engages in activities in a sped up manner	(B) 2 1 0 DK; (R) 2 1 0 DK	?	
70.	Gets up and sits down often or races around the room	(B) 2 1 0 DK; (R) 2 1 0 DK	?	
71.	Is intrusive	(B) 2 1 0 DK; (R) 2 1 0 DK	?	
				Total for Goal Directed Activity Subdomain (B) = ____ (R) = ____
	Excessive Involvement in Pleasurable Activities Subdomain			Notes: None
72.	Engages in sexual behavior or talk	(B) 2 1 0 DK; (R) 2 1 0 DK	?	
73.	Reports a higher rate of sexual activity than usual	(B) 2 1 0 DK; (R) 2 1 0 DK	?	
74.	Masturbates very frequently	(B) 2 1 0 DK; (R) 2 1 0 DK	?	
75.	Exposes himself or herself in public or touches others in a sexual manner	(B) 2 1 0 DK; (R) 2 1 0 DK	?	
				Total for Excessive Involvement in Pleasurable Activities Subdomain (B) = ____ (R) = ____
	Catatonic Features Subdomain			Notes: None
76.	Stands like a statue for long periods of time, or maintains an odd posture	(B) 2 1 0 DK; (R) 2 1 0 DK	?	
77.	Is unresponsive for long periods of time	(B) 2 1 0 DK; (R) 2 1 0 DK	?	
78.	Stereotypic or repetitive behavior increases in intensity or frequency when distressed	(B) 2 1 0 DK; (R) 2 1 0 DK	?	Question is only applicable if stereotypic behavior is present.
				Total for Catatonic Features Subdomain (B) = ____ (R) = ____
	Melancholic Features Subdomain			Notes: A high score on Depression indicates a subtype of melancholic features
79.	Demonstrates more agitated or depressed behavior in the morning than the rest of the day (e.g. tearful, sad)	(B) 2 1 0 DK; (R) 2 1 0 DK	?	
80.	Shows a loss of enjoyment	(B) 2 1 0 DK; (R) 2 1 0 DK	?	
				Total for Melancholic Features Subdomain (B) = ____ (R) = ____
	Atypical Features Subdomain			Notes: None
81.	Sleeps a lot	(B) 2 1 0 DK; (R) 2 1 0 DK	?	
82.	Seeks reassurance or approval from significant others	(B) 2 1 0 DK; (R) 2 1 0 DK	?	

83.	Makes frequent statements about people not liking him or her	(B) 2 1 0 DK; (R) 2 1 0 DK	?	
84.	Is overly sensitive to rejection*	(B) 2 1 0 DK; (R) 2 1 0 DK	?	*Individuals with severe/profound ID are not likely able to express sensitively to rejection in words, but may show these feelings in their behavior.
85.	Expresses feelings of guilt	(B) 2 1 0 DK; (R) 2 1 0 DK	?	
				Total for Atypical Features Subdomain (B) = ___ (R) = ___
Dysthymic Features Subdomain				Notes: None
86.	Struggles with self-esteem in relation to a strong desire to be normal	(B) 2 1 0 DK; (R) 2 1 0 DK	?	
87.	Expresses a sense of hopelessness that the usual accomplishments/ events of adulthood will not happen (e.g., getting a driver's license, getting married)	(B) 2 1 0 DK; (R) 2 1 0 DK	?	
				Total for Dysthymic Features Subdomain (B) = ___ (R) = ___
Panic Subdomain				Notes: For individuals with MILD/ MODErate ID the DM-ID-2 has not adapted the diagnostic criteria. The person may have difficulties with temporal sequencing. To identify one month of time use time frame or anchor events, or description of time frame from informant report.
88.	Appears to become intensely frightened, agitated or intensely distressed abruptly, reaching a peak within minutes	(B) 2 1 0 DK; (R) 2 1 0 DK	?	
89.	Engages in sweating, trembling, or shaking	(B) 2 1 0 DK; (R) 2 1 0 DK	?	
90.	Describes having a pounding or racing heart, or says the chest hurts	(B) 2 1 0 DK; (R) 2 1 0 DK	?	
91.	Gasps for breath, or engages in over breathing or hyperventilating	(B) 2 1 0 DK; (R) 2 1 0 DK	?	
92.	Engages in choking or wheezing	(B) 2 1 0 DK; (R) 2 1 0 DK	?	
93.	Cries or coughs weakly	(B) 2 1 0 DK; (R) 2 1 0 DK	?	
94.	Clutches or rubs the chest or complains of chest pain	(B) 2 1 0 DK; (R) 2 1 0 DK	?	
95.	Complains of nausea, abdominal distress or stomach aches	(B) 2 1 0 DK; (R) 2 1 0 DK	?	
96.	Retches, vomits or has difficulty swallowing	(B) 2 1 0 DK; (R) 2 1 0 DK	?	

97.	Goes "grey," "turns blue," staggers, collapses or has an unsteady gait	(B) 2 1 0 DK; (R) 2 1 0 DK	?	
98.	Complains of chills or hot flushes	(B) 2 1 0 DK; (R) 2 1 0 DK	?	
99.	Becomes irritable or aggressive suddenly	(B) 2 1 0 DK; (R) 2 1 0 DK	?	
100.	Becomes destructive suddenly	(B) 2 1 0 DK; (R) 2 1 0 DK	?	
101.	Lashes out with arms and legs	(B) 2 1 0 DK; (R) 2 1 0 DK	?	
102.	Engages in self-injurious behavior (e.g., head banging)	(B) 2 1 0 DK; (R) 2 1 0 DK	?	
				Total for Panic Subdomain (B) = ____ (R) = ____
	Anxiety/Worry Subdomain			Notes:
103.	Appears anxious or apprehensive	(B) 2 1 0 DK; (R) 2 1 0 DK	?	
104.	Appears needy or clingy	(B) 2 1 0 DK; (R) 2 1 0 DK	?	
105.	Has nightmares associated with fears/anxiety	(B) 2 1 0 DK; (R) 2 1 0 DK	?	
106.	Appears restless or tense (e.g., muscles look tense or facial expression looks tense)	(B) 2 1 0 DK; (R) 2 1 0 DK	?	
107.	Cries, has tantrums, or is difficult to soothe	(B) 2 1 0 DK; (R) 2 1 0 DK	?	
108.	Self-reports worry, anxiety, fears (e.g., says "I'm scared")	(B) 2 1 0 DK; (R) 2 1 0 DK	?	
109.	Reports worries, anxieties and fears even after efforts to soothe	(B) 2 1 0 DK; (R) 2 1 0 DK	?	
				Total for Anxiety/Worry Subdomain (B) = ____ (R) = ____
	Agoraphobia Subdomain			Notes: None
110.	Cries, has a tantrum, freezes or clings in response to being outside the home alone, being in a crowd, standing in a line, being on a bridge or travelling in a bus or car, or refuses to be in these situations*	(B) 2 1 0 DK; (R) 2 1 0 DK	?	*Score if any particular situations cause panic.
				Total for Agoraphobia Subdomain (B) = ____ (R) = ____
	Specific Phobia Subdomain			Notes: None
111.	Cries, has a tantrum, freezes or clings in response to specific objects or situations*	(B) 2 1 0 DK; (R) 2 1 0 DK	?	* Most often seen in individuals with severe ID.
				Total for Specific Phobia Subdomain (B) = ____ (R) = ____

	Social Phobia Subdomain			Notes: Duration of symptoms must be at least 6 months in individuals with ID in order to give points for this subdomain.
112.	Fears social situations (e.g. going places with others)	(B) 2 1 0 DK; (R) 2 1 0 DK	?	
113.	Cries, freezes, or clings in social situations*	(B) 2 1 0 DK; (R) 2 1 0 DK	?	*Most often seen in individuals with severe ID.
				Total for Social Phobia Subdomain (B) = ___ (R) = ___
	Social Deficits Subdomain			Notes: None
114.	Rejects interaction or seeks to prolong it	(B) 2 1 0 DK; (R) 2 1 0 DK	?	
115.	Actively avoids eye contact	(B) 2 1 0 DK; (R) 2 1 0 DK	?	
116.	Actively isolates himself or herself from peers	(B) 2 1 0 DK; (R) 2 1 0 DK	?	
				Total for Social Deficits Subdomain (B) = ___ (R) = ___
	Stereotypical Behaviors Subdomain			Notes: Repetitive, seemingly driven behavior without obsessions or cognitive symptoms.
117.	Reacts catastrophically (like it's the end of the world) to changes in routine or environment	(B) 2 1 0 DK; (R) 2 1 0 DK	?	
118.	Engages in hand shaking, waving, body rocking, head banging, mouthing, self-biting or hitting own body	(B) 2 1 0 DK; (R) 2 1 0 DK	?	
119.	Toe-walks (walk on their tip toes) or twirls (twirls in circles)	(B) 2 1 0 DK; (R) 2 1 0 DK	?	
				Total for Stereotypical behaviors Subdomain (B) = ___ (R) = ___
	Echolalia Subdomain			Notes: The presence of echolalia can indicate an autism spectrum disorder and/or a tic disorder. If there was a loss of language after age 3 refer for epilepsy screening.
120.	Repeats words or phrases and/or imitates others (Echolalia)*	(B) 2 1 0 DK; (R) 2 1 0 DK	?	* Individuals with severe/profound ID are more likely to imitate the behavior of others. There is a waxing and waning of behaviors often paralleling a flare up in motor skills.
121.	Echolalia increases during times of distress	(B) 2 1 0 DK; (R) 2 1 0 DK	?	

			Total for Echolalia Subdomain (B) = ___ (R) = ___
Simple Tics Subdomain			Notes: Complete this subdomain only for individuals with severe/profound ID. Akathisia and restless leg syndrome must be ruled out. See notes for motor tics mild/moderate ID.
122.	Engages in repetitive physical movements such as eye-blinking, nose-twitching, head-jerking, shoulder-shrugging, or facial grimacing*	(B) 2 1 0 DK; (R) 2 1 0 DK	?	* More commonly seen in severe/profound ID. In general there is a waxing and waning course of target behaviors. Not an exhaustive list, score if simple motor tics are present that involve brief repetitive movements and a limited number of muscle groups.
123.	Engages in sudden or quick aggressive or violent behaviors (explosions at the same time as repetitive physical movements (motor tics)*	(B) 2 1 0 DK; (R) 2 1 0 DK	?	
124.	Engages in self-injurious behavior (hurting self) in the presence of repetitive physical movements*	(B) 2 1 0 DK; (R) 2 1 0 DK	?	*More commonly seen in severe/profound ID. In general there is a waxing and waning course of target behaviors.
				Total for Simple Tics Severe/Profound ID Subdomain (B) = ___ (R) = ___
Serious Self-Injurious Behavior Subdomain			Notes: Severe self-injurious behaviors are usually associated with severe tics and sensory phenomena.
125.	Engages in self-injurious behavior (e.g., hits self, scratches self, or bites self)	(B) 2 1 0 DK; (R) 2 1 0 DK	?	
				Total for Serious Self-Injurious Behaviors Subdomain (B) = ___ (R) = ___
Sensory Tics Subdomain			Notes: Sensory tics are unwanted or uncomfortable sensations. Complete this subdomain only for individuals with mild/moderate ID.
126.	Complains of uncomfortable feelings such as tickling, warmth, cold or pressure in the body (e.g. in the throat, eyes, or shoulders)	(B) 2 1 0 DK; (R) 2 1 0 DK	?	
				Total for Sensory Tics Mild/Moderate ID Subdomain (B) = ___ (R) = ___
Minor Self-injurious Behaviors Subdomain			Notes: Minor tics are usually high frequency and low intensity.
127.	Engages in nose picking, cuticle or nail pulling or manipulates minor skin causing tissue damage	(B) 2 1 0 DK; (R) 2 1 0 DK	?	

			Total for Minor Self-Injurious Behaviors Subdomain (B) = ____ (R) = ____
	Phonic Tics Subdomain		Notes: None
128.	Vocalizes in an abrupt or explosive manner such as coughing, grunting, or barking	(B) 2 1 0 DK; (R) 2 1 0 DK	?
129.	Abrupt or explosive vocalizations become more severe when distressed	(B) 2 1 0 DK; (R) 2 1 0 DK	?
130.	Repeats the end of his or her sentences (Pallilalia)	(B) 2 1 0 DK; (R) 2 1 0 DK	?
131.	Swears or uses obscene words without intensive affective response to pain or anger (Coprolalia)	(B) 2 1 0 DK; (R) 2 1 0 DK	?
132.	Engages in continuous complex tics, such as humming	(B) 2 1 0 DK; (R) 2 1 0 DK	?
			Total for Phonic Tics Mild/Moderate Subdomain (B) = ____ (R) = ____
	Complex Tics Subdomain		Notes: Distinct coordinated patterns of movement involving several muscle groups.
133.	Engages in sniffing, hopping, jumping, bending, twisting, facial grimacing, head twisting, or shoulder shrugging*	(B) 2 1 0 DK; (R) 2 1 0 DK	?	*Not an exhaustive list, score if any pattern of movement is present that involves several muscle groups.
			?	Total for Complex Tics Subdomain (B) = ____ (R) = ____
	Motor Tics Subdomain		Notes: Abnormal movements are often confused with seizure disorders, tardive dyskinesia, or provocative gesturing. The use of anti-psychotic drugs can suppress pre-existing tics. Tics, SIB, and altered mood states can be confused with metabolic disorders such as Lesch-Nyhan syndrome or degenerative disorders such as Huntingdon's disease leading to inaccurate diagnoses and interventions.
134.	Engages in counting	(B) 2 1 0 DK; (R) 2 1 0 DK	?	
135.	Describes symptoms such as a tingling, cramping or funny feelings in an area of the body that is associated with an urge to move*	(B) 2 1 0 DK; (R) 2 1 0 DK	?	* The urge to move is relieved when the person gives in to the urge to move.

136.	Aligns objects or needs to arrange items symmetrically	(B) 2 1 0 DK; (R) 2 1 0 DK	?	
137.	Touches objects or body parts repeatedly	(B) 2 1 0 DK; (R) 2 1 0 DK	?	
				Total for Motor Tics Subdomain (B) = ___ (R) = ___
	Minor Self-injurious Behaviors Subdomain			Notes: Minor tics are usually high frequency and low intensity.
138.	Engages in nose picking, cuticle or nail pulling, or manipulates skin causing tissue damage	(B) 2 1 0 DK; (R) 2 1 0 DK	?	
				Total for Minor Self-Injurious Behaviors Subdomain (B) = ___ (R) = ___
	Phonic Tics Subdomain			
139.	Vocalizes in an explosive manner exacerbated by distress*	(B) 2 1 0 DK; (R) 2 1 0 DK	?	*Waxing and waning of behaviors often parallel a flare up in motor tics.
140.	Engages in imitative behaviors or Echolalia*	(B) 2 1 0 DK; (R) 2 1 0 DK	?	
				Total for Phonic Tics (B) = ___ (R) = ___
	Hallucinations/Psychosis Subdomain			Notes: Consider developmental profile/cognition of the examinee. Reality and fantasy distinctions are often poor. Individuals with ID may use fantasy to cope with stress, engage in self-talk or to express odd or intense fears. Trauma-specific enactments have been observed in adults with moderate to severe ID and can appear to be symptoms of psychosis in adults.
141.	Sees things that are not there, such as ghosts or monsters	(B) 2 1 0 DK; (R) 2 1 0 DK	?	
142.	Talks conversationally when alone or has conversations with imaginary voices	(B) 2 1 0 DK; (R) 2 1 0 DK	?	
143.	Hears voices that tell the person to do things such as engage in destructive behavior or make the person feel afraid	(B) 2 1 0 DK; (R) 2 1 0 DK	?	
144.	Experiences a change in verbal fluency (talks less or more)*	(B) 2 1 0 DK; (R) 2 1 0 DK	?	*Only answer this question if the examinee is verbal.
145.	Shows change in mood, speech, or volition (choices) that are not reasonable for the situation	(B) 2 1 0 DK; (R) 2 1 0 DK	?	
145.	Is socially withdrawn or engages in stereotypical/odd behavior	(B) 2 1 0 DK; (R) 2 1 0 DK	?	

146.	Behaves fearfully	(B) 2 1 0 DK; (R) 2 1 0 DK	?	
147.	Shows gradual deterioration in functioning	(B) 2 1 0 DK; (R) 2 1 0 DK	?	
				Total for Hallucinations/Psychosis Subdomain (B) = ___ (R) = ___
	Post-Traumatic/Acute Stress Subdomain			Notes: Trauma specific enactments have been observed in individuals with moderate to severe ID. These episodes require judicious assessment since they can appear to be symptoms of psychosis in adults. Anxiety and depression may manifest in persons with mild/moderate ID as they would in persons without ID. Consider if factors such as a chronic disabling general medical condition, unrelieved inappropriate educational, residential or vocational placement, repeated caregiver turnover, unrelieved peer problem exposure, or other experiences beyond the capacity of the individual to resolve independently are present.
148.	Has frightening dreams with or without recognizable content*	(B) 2 1 0 DK; (R) 2 1 0 DK	?	
149.	Shows diminished interest in participating in activities (caregivers often describe this behavior as noncompliance)	(B) 2 1 0 DK; (R) 2 1 0 DK	?	*Individuals with ID may not be able to describe dream content, or explain that they are having bad dreams. Behavioral observations in these cases may include difficulty staying asleep or getting up early.
150.	Isolates self from others	(B) 2 1 0 DK; (R) 2 1 0 DK	?	
151.	Displays self-injurious, disorganized, agitated, or aggressive behavior*	(B) 2 1 0 DK; (R) 2 1 0 DK	?	*Primarily in individuals with a lower cognitive functioning. For people with ID, this may also be observed as an increase in the frequency or severity of pre-existing maladaptive behavioral repertoires.
				Total for PTSD Subdomain (B) = ___ (R) = ___
	Attachment Subdomain			Notes: To score symptoms must have begun before age 5 and person must have a developmental level of 9 months. If onset of symptoms is unknown this subdomain cannot be completed. Autism spectrum disorder and reactive attachment disorder are able to be distinguished through the quality of communication, presence or absence of repetitive behaviors or interests, etc.
152.	Has difficulty establishing/ maintaining eye contact	(B) 2 1 0 DK; (R) 2 1 0 DK	?	
153.	Rarely or minimally seeks comfort when distressed	(B) 2 1 0 DK; (R) 2 1 0 DK	?	

154.	Seeks personal closeness in an impaired or indiscriminant (non-selective) way when distressed or in pain	(B) 2 1 0 DK; (R) 2 1 0 DK	?	
155.	Demonstrates impaired ability to relate to parents, peers, or caregivers	(B) 2 1 0 DK; (R) 2 1 0 DK	?	
156.	Demonstrates an impaired reaction to the absence of preferred caregivers	(B) 2 1 0 DK; (R) 2 1 0 DK	?	
157.	Demonstrates impaired or aggressive behavior upon the return of caregivers	(B) 2 1 0 DK; (R) 2 1 0 DK	?	
158.	Has a history of abuse or neglect during infancy, childhood, and/or adulthood	(B) 2 1 0 DK; (R) 2 1 0 DK	?	
159.	Actively approaches unfamiliar adults or overly verbal or physical behavior.	(B) 2 1 0 DK; (R) 2 1 0 DK	?	
160.	Willing to leave with an unfamiliar adult with minimal or without hesitation.	(B) 2 1 0 DK; (R) 2 1 0 DK	?	
				Total for Attachment Subdomain (B) = ____ (R) = ____
	Compulsions Subdomain			Notes: Repetitive behaviors may not cause distress or anxiety. The function of the behavior may not be ascertainable.
161.	Engages in ordering, hoarding, telling, asking, or rubbing*	(B) 2 1 0 DK; (R) 2 1 0 DK	?	*Behavioral observations more typical of individuals with mild/ moderate ID.
162.	Insists on fixed sequences, arranges or orders objects compulsively, or fills or empty objects compulsively*	(B) 2 1 0 DK; (R) 2 1 0 DK	?	*Behavioral observations more typical of individuals with severe/ profound ID.
163.	Engages in aggression or self-injurious behavior if completion of compulsion is prevented	(B) 2 1 0 DK; (R) 2 1 0 DK	?	
				Total for Compulsions Subdomain (B) = ____ (R) = ____

DM-ID-2 Workbook Scoring Sheets

Instructions: Copy the Baseline (B) and Recent (R) scores from the Interview Questions Form onto the table for each of the 12 domains listed below. Once all the scores have been transferred to the tables on the scoring sheet, turn to the instructions below each table regarding the use of decision trees, starting at Table 1, and continuing through to Table 11 to ensure all possible diagnoses are considered. A space is provided at the end of the scoring sheet to note all possible diagnoses indicated by decision trees.

Table 1: Depressive Disorders Domain

Subdomains	Total Score for Baseline Behavior	Total Score for Recent Behavior
Depression		
Irritability/Aggression		
General Behavior		
Weight/ Appetite		
Insomnia		
Hypersomnia		
Psychomotor Agitation		
Psychomotor Retardation		
Fatigue/ Energy Loss		
Worthlessness/ Excessive Inappropriate Guilt		
Diminished Ability to Concentrate		
Distractibility		
Recurrent Thoughts of Death/ Suicidal Ideation		
Catatonic Features		
Melancholic Features		
Atypical Features		
Dysthymic Features		

Instructions for Table 1: Turn to Decision Tree A _only_ if the examinee has a score of at least 1 point in one of the subdomains of the Depressive Disorder Domain.

Table 2: Mania or Hypomania Domain

Subdomains	Total Score for Baseline Behavior	Total Score for Recent Behavior
Mania		
Inflated Self-Esteem/ Grandiosity		
Decreased Need for Sleep		
Talkative/ Pressure to Talk		
Goal Directed Activity		
Excessive Involvement in Pleasurable Activity		

Instructions for Table 2: Turn to Decision Tree B _only_ if the examinee has a score of at least 1 point in the Mania subdomain _and_ at least 1 point in two or more other subdomains. If criteria are met for both Decision Tree A and B based on scores in the Depressive and Manic or Hypomanic Domain, turn to Decision Tree C, because a bipolar diagnosis may be present.

Table 3: Panic Disorders Domain

Subdomains	Total Score for Baseline Behavior	Total Score for Recent Behavior
Panic		
Agoraphobia		
Specific Phobia		
Social Phobia		
Minor Self-Injurious Behavior		

Instructions for Table 3: Turn to Decision Tree D _only_ if there is a score of at least 1 point in the Panic Subdomain. Scores in other subdomains can be used to inform differential diagnosis.

Table 4: Anxiety Disorders Domain

Subdomains	Total Score for Baseline Behavior	Total Score for Recent Behavior
Anxiety/Worry		
Fatigue/ Energy Loss		
Diminished Ability to Concentrate		
Irritability/Aggression		
Insomnia		
Hypersomnia		

Instructions for Table 4: Turn to Decision Tree E _only_ if there is at least 1 point in Anxiety/ Worry and at least one other subdomain in the Anxiety Disorder domain.

Table 5: Autism Spectrum Disorders Domain

Subdomains	Total Score for Baseline Behavior	Total Score for Recent Behavior
Social Deficits		
Stereotypical Behaviors		
Echolalia		

Instructions for Table 5: Turn to Decision Tree F _only_ if there is a total score of at least 1 point in a subdomain of this domain.

Table 6: Stereotypic Movement Disorder Domain

Subdomains	Total Score for Baseline Behavior	Total Score for Recent Behavior
Simple Tics Severe		
Serious Self-Injurious Behavior		

Instructions for Table 6: Turn to Decision Tree G _only_ if there is a score of at least 1 point in each subdomain.

Table 7: Tic Disorders Domain

Subdomains	Total Score for Baseline Behavior	Total Score for Recent Behavior
Sensory Tics		
Minor Self-Injurious Behavior		
Phonic Tics		
Complex Tics		
Serious Self-Injurious Behaviors		
Phonic Tics		
Simple Tics		

Instructions for Table 8: Turn to Decision Tree H _only_ if there is a score of at least 1 point in this domain.

Table 8: Psychotic Disorders Domain

Subdomain	Total Score for Baseline Behavior	Total Score for Recent Behavior
Hallucinations		

Instructions for Table 8: Turn to Decision Tree I _only_ if there is a score of at least 1 point in the Hallucinations subdomain. Note that if hallucinations are present at the same time as mood symptoms, a mood disorder diagnosis with a subtype of psychotic features should be considered. To differentiate between Schizophrenia and Mood Disorders the onset of symptoms must be considered, e.g., insidious or acute onset.

Table 9: Attention Deficit and Hyperactivity Disorder, Post-Traumatic Stress Disorder, Acute Stress Disorder Domain

Subdomains	Total Score for Baseline Behavior	Total Score for Recent Behavior
Posttraumatic Stress		
Irritability/Aggression		
Diminished Ability to Concentrate		
Distractibility		
Psychomotor Agitation		
Talkative/ Pressure to Talk		
Goal Directed Activity		
Decreased Need for Sleep		

Instructions for Table 9:

1) Turn to Decision Tree J and K if there is a score of at least 1 point or more in any subdomains in this domain.
2) Turn to Decision Tree J, K, _and_ A if the person has a score of at least 1 point or more in at least one or more of the following subdomains: Posttraumatic Stress, Irritability/ Aggression, Diminished Ability to Concentrate, and Distractibility, because a differential diagnosis will need to be made between ADHD, PTSD and Depressive Disorders (unless as mentioned in step one there is only a score in the Posttraumatic Stress subdomain and no other subdomains). Note that Post Traumatic Stress Disorder is extremely common in individuals with ID, and developmental level should be taken into consideration when determining if the examinee has been affected by trauma.
3) Turn to Decision Tree J _and_ A) if there is a score of at least 1 point in the Psychomotor Agitation subdomain because this observable behavior is found in individuals with ADHD and Depression.
4) Turn to decision tree J _and_ B if the individual has a score of at least 1 point in the Talkativeness, Goal Directed Activity, or Decreased Need for Sleep subdomains, because a differential diagnosis will need to be made between ADHD and disorders involving mania.
5) Turn to Decision Tree J _and_ C if the individual has at least 1 point in two or more of the Attention Deficit and Hyperactivity Disorder/ Posttraumatic Stress Disorder subdomains, because a differential diagnosis will need to be made between Bipolar Disorder and ADHD.

Table 10: Reactive Attachment/Disinhibited Social Engagement Disorder Domain

Subdomain	Total Score for Baseline Behavior	Total Score for Recent Behavior
Attachment		

Instructions for Table 10: There is no corresponding decision tree for this domain. If at least 1 point is scored in this subdomain, turn to the *DM-ID*-2 to determine if a Reactive Attachment Disorder or Disinhibited Social Engagement Disorder should be diagnosed.

Table 11: Compulsive Disorder Domain

Subdomain	Total Score for Baseline Behavior	Total Score for Recent Behavior
Compulsions		

Instructions for Table 11: There is no corresponding decision tree for this domain. If at least 1 point is scored in this subdomain, turn to the *DM-ID*-2 to determine if an Obsessive-Compulsive Disorder should be diagnosed.

All possible applicable diagnoses should be noted below. Clinicians should review the diagnostic criteria for each applicable diagnosis in the *DM-ID*-2 to ensure that no mutually exclusive diagnoses are given and the best possible diagnoses are given.

_____

_____

_____

_____

_____

_____

_____

_____

_____

_____

_____

_____

_____

_____

_____

_____

_____

_____

_____

_____

DM-ID-2 Workbook Decision Trees

There are a total of 11 decision trees that correspond to the 11 domains described earlier. Each decision tree has a list of diagnoses that may, or may not, be relevant to the individual. Instructions on the scoring sheet below the table for each domain indicate whether or not the diagnoses on a particular decision tree should be considered for the examinee.

Decision Tree A

· Major depressive disorder (consider diagnosing with catatonia, melancholic features, or atypical features if the examinee scored more highly in one of these subdomains compared to the others).
· Disruptive mood dysregulation disorder
· Persistent depressive disorder (dysthymia)
· Adjustment disorder with depressed mood
· Premenstrual dysphoric disorder
· Substance/medication-induced depressive disorder
· Depressive disorder due to another medical condition
· Other specified depressive disorder
· Unspecified depressive disorder

Decision Tree B

· Manic episode
· Hypomanic episode
· Bipolar I disorder, single manic episode

Decision Tree C

· Bipolar I disorder
· Bipolar II disorder
· Cyclothymic disorder
· Substance/medication-induced bipolar and related disorder
· Bipolar and related disorder due to another medical condition
· Other specified bipolar and related disorder
· Unspecified bipolar and related disorder

Decision Tree D

· Specific phobia
· Social anxiety disorder (social phobia)
· Panic disorder
· Panic attack
· Agoraphobia

Decision Tree E

· Generalized anxiety disorder
· Substance/medication-induced anxiety disorder
· Anxiety disorder due to another medical condition
· Other specified anxiety disorder
· Unspecified anxiety disorder
· Adjustment disorder with anxiety
· Adjustment disorder with disturbance of conduct

37

Decision Tree F
· Autism spectrum disorder

Decision Tree G
· Stereotypic movement disorder

Decision Tree H
· Persistent (chronic) motor or vocal disorder
· Transient tic disorder
· Provisional tic disorder
· Other specified tic disorder unspecified tic disorder

Decision Tree I
· Schizotypal (personality disorder)
· Delusional disorder
· Brief psychotic disorder
· Schizophrenia
· Schizophreniform disorder
· Schizoaffective disorder
· Psychotic disorder due to another medical condition
· Other specified schizophrenia spectrum and other psychotic disorder
· Unspecified schizophrenia spectrum and other psychotic disorder
· Catatonia (including three subtypes):
  o Catatonia associated with another mental disorder (catatonia specifier)
  o Catatonic disorder due to another medical condition
  o Unspecified catatonia
· Major depressive disorder with psychotic features
· Bipolar disorder with psychotic features

Decision Tree J
· Attention deficit/hyper activity disorder

Decision Tree K
· Posttraumatic stress disorder
· Acute stress disorder
· Other trauma- and stressor-related disorder
· Unspecified trauma- and stressor-related disorder

References

American Educational Research Association, American Psychological Association, & National Council on Measurement in Education. (1999). *Standards in educational and psychological testing.* Washington, DC: Author

Einfield, S. L. (1992). Clinical assessment of psychiatric symptoms in mentally retarded individuals. *Australian and New Zealand Journal of Psychiatry, 26*, 48-63.

Einfield, S. L., & Aman, M. G. (1995). Issue in the taxonomy of psychopathology in children and adolescents with mental retardation. *Journal of Autism and Developmental Disorders, 25*, 143-167.

Fletcher, R., Loschen, E., Stavrakaki, C., & First, M. (Eds.). (2007). *Diagnostic manual- intellectual disability: A textbook of diagnosis of mental disorders in persons with intellectual disability.* Kingston, NY: NADD Press.

Gustafsson, C., & Sonnander, K. (2004). Occurrence of mental health problems in Swedish samples of adults with intellectual disabilities. *Social Psychiatry and Psychiatric Epidemiology, 39*, 448-456.

Laman, D.S., & Reiss, S. (1987). Social skill deficiencies associated with depressed mood of mentally retarded adults. *American Journal of Mental Deficiency, 92*, 224-229.

Moss, S., Emerson, E., Bouras, N., & Holland, A. (1997). Mental disorders and problematic behaviours in people with intellectual disability: Future directions for research. *Journal of Intellectual Disability Research Mental Health and Intellectual Disability, 41(6)*, 440-447.

Moss, S., Prosser, H., Costello, H., Simpson, N., Patel, P., & Rowe, S. (1998). Reliability and validity of the PAS-ADD Checklist for detecting psychiatric disorders in adults with intellectual disability. *Journal of Intellectual Disability Research, 42(2)*, 173-183.

Poindexter, A. (1996). Current trends in mental health care for persons with mental retardation. *The Journal of Rehabilitation.* Retrieved from: http://www.thefreelibrary.com/ Current+trends+in+mental+health+care+for+persons+with+mental...-a018562555

Reiss, S. (1990). Prevalence of dual diagnosis in community-based day programs in the Chicago metropolitan area. *American Journal on Mental Retardation, 94*, 578-585.

Reiss, S. (1993). Assessment of psychopathology in persons with mental retardation. In J. L. Matson & R. P. Barrett, R, P. (Eds.), *Psychopathology in the mentally retarded* (2nd ed.,pp. 17-40). Needham Heights, MA; Allyn & Bacon.

Rush, A.J., & Frances, A. (Eds.). (2000). Treatment of psychiatric and behavioral   problems in mental retardation (Special Issue). *American Journal on Mental Retardation, 105(3)*, 165-226.

Sovner, R., & Pary, R. J. (1993). Affective disorders in developmentally disabled persons. In J. L. Matson & R. P. Barrett (Eds.). *Psychopathology in the mentally retarded* (2nd ed.,pp. 87-148). Needham Heights, MA; Allyn & Bacon.